INTERVIEWS

MICHAEL FORSTER

To Amity U.R.C.
with best wishes
Michael Forster

Kevin
Mayhew

First published in 1997 by
KEVIN MAYHEW LTD
Rattlesden
Bury St Edmunds
Suffolk IP30 0SZ

0 1 2 3 4 5 6 7 8 9

ISBN 0 86209 977 3
Catalogue No 1500102

Cover illustration by Eddy Mooney
Edited by David Gatward
Typesetting by Louise Hill
Printed and bound in Great Britain

Contents

Contents

Foreword

We at Kevin Mayhew Publishers, at great expense and considerable personal risk, have been able to infiltrate the archives of Megabucks Television and secure access to these hitherto unpublished transcripts of an exclusive series of interviews between their top chat show host, Theodore (Theo) Logian, and God.

Well, that's the official story. The unofficial one (leaked to the media by a junior executive at Megabucks who has since been moved to a more senior and therefore less sensitive post) is that the interviews were concocted by a writer seeking a fresh way of presenting religious issues. Some authors, of course, will do anything for a new angle and this version may therefore be at least as credible as the official one . . .

Whichever account of events is true, we hope the scripts may be interesting and useful. They might perhaps be used in place of sermons in worship services, or perhaps in youth groups or schools. If so, then the following notes might be helpful.

The relationship between the interviewer and Big G is very important. Although initially reticent (and who wouldn't be?) Logian finds his confidence fairly quickly. He is a person of faith and is soon able to relax and engage in banter with his distinguished interviewee. The atmosphere is good humoured and open, as between friends who trust one another.

As the relationship and Logian's confidence grow, Big G feels it appropriate to become incarnate in different forms. Logian responds to this in various ways and sometimes the repartee becomes sharper, but never hostile. Big G often presents a challenge to his interviewer, but their friendship and mutual trust are never in doubt.

First Encounter

Logian   Good evening and welcome to another edition of *On the Spot*, the programme where the movers, the shakers and the shapers of destiny get theirs. Our interviewers have been accused in the past of bullying, hectoring, threatening and even blackmailing the poor defenceless generals and politicians who have dared to sit in the 'Big Red Chair'. Tonight's guest, though, only agreed to be interviewed *on condition* that he should be accorded no special treatment. More popular, some say, than the Beatles, Frank Bruno and Doris the canteen manager put together, he is variously described by others as a fraud, a megalomaniac or even an illusion. Known over thousands of years by such names as Adonai, Jehovah, Yahweh and the Great I Am, to name but a few, he is of course: God. Welcome to *On the Spot*; it's a real privilege for us.

God   Thank you, Theo. It's a very great pleasure for me, too.

Logian   I suppose the first thing I must ask is, what would you like me to call you?

God   That's an excellent question, Theo. The different names people call me have caused so much suffering, I'm grateful for the chance to talk about that.

Logian   Very well, so which one is right?

God   Do I really have to say that just one is right and all the rest are wrong?

Logian	In view of what you've just said, I think it might be an excellent idea. But if it helps, tell me which one you *prefer*.
God	That's almost as difficult. What I *prefer* is not to go by any name in particular, but I realise that it's a bit impractical.
Logian	Why's that?
God	It's not easy to explain. Look, d'you mind if I use your name as an illustration?
Logian	Yes, that's fine.
God	Thank you. Right: Theodore Logian. *Theo* Logian. Now if I didn't know you really well (which of course I do) and if I went in for stereotypes (which of course I don't but bear with me for a moment) then I might think you were, say, a highbrow academic . . .
Logian	Hardly.
God	. . . living in Oxford or Cambridge in an ivory tower . . .
Logian	I got sent down.
God	. . . with an enquiring mind?
Logian	Ah! I'd like to think that one's right.
God	Well, one out of three's not bad, you might say, and it's better than some people do when they try to interpret the labels they've stuck on me.

Logian   I'm not sure I follow.

God   Let's see, then. Some people call me 'Lord', and that's alright until they start treating me like some feudal baron to whom everybody should touch the forelock and cringe obsequiously. Then again, 'Mighty God' sounds quite appropriate, as long as they don't expect me to throw thunderbolts the way a naughty child throws tantrums in order to get my way. 'King' is a popular name people give to me; they sometimes give it to their dogs, as well, and I do believe there's even a variety of fast food called a 'king burger', so perhaps that's not so helpful, either. Then there's 'Ruler of the Universe'. Apart from having the same problems as 'Lord,' that one also seems to mean that people can use me to draw lines on maps and straighten out other people's lives.

Logian   Well, perhaps I should just settle for 'God'. Then we can proceed with the interview.

God   Yes, I'm sorry to hold you up, Theo, but as you rightly said it's an important question. Look, why don't you just call me Big G?

Logian   I'm sorry?

God   Nothing to apologise for, Theo.

Logian   No, I meant I don't understand.

God   Don't understand what? Oh, 'Big G'? Rather nice, isn't it? It's what Gabriel calls me when he forgets I'm omniscient and thinks my back's turned.

Logian	And you tolerate that kind of disrespect from subordinates, do you?
God	Oh, I *love* it! Life would be so much better for all of us if people would be more natural when they know I'm around (which I always am). Anyway, I've been called a lot worse things than that. I'm really not so concerned with people being polite to me as I am about their being considerate towards each other.
Logian	But doesn't it hurt if people insult you? Or does your divine nature protect you from such things?
God	O come on, Theo! Have you looked at a crucifix recently? Of course it hurts, but if they do it to me directly then only I have to suffer it. It's when they do or say hurtful things to each other – often to people who can't handle it. Then those people get hurt; and because they're hurt, I end up suffering even more.
Logian	I suppose that actually makes a lot of sense.
God	Coming from someone of your standing in the media, Theo, I value the compliment.
Logian	You're welcome. Now, where was I?
God	You were about to ask me about the state of the world.
Logian	Yes. How did you know?
Big G	Just a lucky guess, I suppose. Hadn't you better just ask the question?
Logian	Well, since you know it already . . .

Big G   I'm sure the viewers would like to hear it, unless they've guessed it, too, of course – both of them.

Logian   Big G: are we correct in regarding you as the creator of the world?

Big G   We'll probably need to unpack that a little – but in simple terms, yes.

Logian   Then I'm sure you will have heard it said – and you realise that I must ask you this for the sake of the viewers – that if a car is always going wrong then the manufacturer has to take some responsibility for it.

Big G   Yes, I've heard that said.

Logian   So? What do you think of it?

Big G   Absolutely. But since when was I a car manufacturer?

Logian   Well you're not, of course – or not directly, anyway – but the same principle applies.

Big G   Oh, I see. You think I should have made the world like a kind of cosmic mechanical conveyance, so that I would always be in the driving seat?

Logian   It's a point of view.

Big G   And a very good one, too. Theo, d'you mind if I speak frankly?

Logian   Not at all, Big G.

Big G   I think we'd get on better with this if you

	forgot that I'm Big G and thought of me as a politician.
Logian	I'm not sure I follow you.
Big G	I can't help noticing that you're usually a lot harder on them than you're being on me.
Logian	Well, of course – you're . . .
Big G	That's the point, Theo. There's no question you can't ask me; nothing I'm afraid of; nothing I'm going to try and wriggle out of, or blame you for asking. So *be an interviewer*. The question you're really asking is, if I made the world, why is it such an awful place, and why don't I do something about it?
Logian	Saints preserve me from omniscient guests! I had this trouble with Mrs. T.
Big G	So do I, Theo, and believe me I sympathise. But that was the question, wasn't it?
Logian	That was what I was getting at, yes.
Big G	It's a good question, and my first answer is that the world's *not* really a bad place. It's a very good place with quite a lot wrong with it.
Logian	So you accept that there's a lot wrong?
Big G	Of course I do.
Logian	And you accept responsibility?
Big G	That's a very cold question, Theo. But yes, I accept that I have some responsibility.

Logian   Accepting *some* responsibility is not the same as saying it's your fault, is it? (You did tell me to treat you like a politician.)

Big G   That's fine, Theo. You just keep on going. You're determined to get at the truth, and I'm very keen to help you, which makes us a pretty good double act, I'd say.

Logian   So where do we go now?

Big G   What would you ask the Prime Minister?

Logian   I'd ask whether all these problems weren't the sign of an uncaring government.

Big G   Now *that's* the real question.

Logian   So I'm asking it, Big G. Don't you care about the world?

Big G   Passionately, Theo. And much too much to make it into a machine. I want to be a *creator* not an engineer. I want to have a relationship with my creation: love and be loved, not just automatically obeyed.

Logian   So you're not in charge of events, then? Creation is just free to do its own thing? Is that what you're saying?

Big G   It's about as free as you are, Theo. Tell me, do you and your wife control one another?

Logian   No. But I must remind you that I'm supposed to be asking the questions.

Big G   Humour me a minute, Theo. Sometimes you

have to ask a question to answer one – my Son's always doing it. Now, how do you and Fiona manage things and make decisions?

Logian   Well, we talk a lot.

Big G   And very well it works, too, on the whole. But suppose you really wanted Fiona to do a particular thing, take up gardening, for example, but she didn't want to?

Logian   I'm trying – I mean *I'd try* to persuade her.

Big G   Right. And in this highly hypothetical situation, what if she refuses?

Logian   Well, I can't make her, can I?

Big G   Why not? You're physically bigger and stronger than she is, and you earn a lot more – although I'm working on that, along with other injustices. You could pressurise her, coerce her, bully her a little.

Logian   Really, Big G, you can't be serious. She's my wife, not an interviewee.

Big G   Precisely. So neither of you actually controls the other; you're both quite free, but neither of you is *totally* free because you want to have a relationship. You accept the limitations of that, and try to use the love you share to persuade each other.

Logian   I suppose that's right.

Big G   So why shouldn't I have that sort of relationship with the world?

Logian   Can't you do both? You've got infinite power, haven't you?

Big G   Even I can't make a square circle, or dry wetness. Still less can I create a robot that can't think for itself and yet is free, and most importantly, capable of loving.

Logian   So are you telling me you haven't got power, then?

Big G   There's a big difference between having power and using it, Theo. There are many times when I'd like to put people on a lead, like pets, and control them. But I always resist it.

Logian   Look, Big G, talking about freedom's all very well, but some people would say that all your neat academic arguments don't amount to a hill of beans compared with the price some people seem to be paying for it.

Big G   Freedom's expensive; you're quite right – because it's meaningless unless your bad choices have consequences, as well as your good ones.

Logian   That's a nice argument but it avoids the issue. The point is: why do the *innocent* have to suffer the painful consequences of *other people's* freedom?

Big G   Well, I could create for you a world where you could behave as you liked and no one else would be affected.

Logian   Sounds great! How would you do that?

Big G   Simple. There'd be no one else in it.

Logian	Not even Fiona, and Luke and Dan?
Big G	Not unless you want to take the risk of hurting them.
Logian	I don't think I'd like to be all alone, however beautiful the world was.
Big G	I agree with you – it'd be ghastly, wouldn't it? But if you were to have freedom, and at the same time make sure that your actions didn't harm anyone else, then you'd simply have to live in a world all your own.
Logian	So let me get this straight, Big G. You're happy to accept that, in the interests of freedom and relationships, innocent people are going to get hurt and it's a price worth paying?
Big G	*[Horrified]* No, Theo, I'm not happy about it; I hate it. But if I want people to love one another – and I want that more than anything else – then I can't isolate them, can I?
Logian	But you must have an answer to the problem.
Big G	Yes, I have. but it's neither quick nor easy. Perhaps you'd like to tell me what *you* think I should do?
Logian	It's happening again. You seem to be interviewing me more than I am you.
Big G	That's alright. I'll let you keep the fee. Now, tell me, Theo, if your children were quarrelling all the time . . .
Logian	'If!'

Big G   Oh, don't exaggerate, Theo. Well, what do you do about it? Have you locked them away in separate houses, yet?

Logian   No, I hadn't thought of that.

Big G   No, and I hope you won't. What do you actually want to happen, Theo?

Logian   I want them to learn to live together better.

Big G   So how are they going to learn that?

Logian   I suppose by doing it.

Big G   Bullseye! Now, while they're learning by doing, how do you feel when they're quarrelling, or when one of them's unhappy?

Logian   It hurts like hell.

Big G   A most appropriate simile, if I may say so. So what can you do?

Logian   All we seem able to do is hang in there: try to show them better ways, keep on loving them, and hope they'll change.

Big G   You're a good parent, Theo. And do they know you're hurting?

Logian   I think they're gradually realising it and making an effort to change.

Big G   Something tells me that in answering my questions you've begun to answer your own. I must remember to congratulate Jesus on this technique. It's really very good.

Logian   A good note on which to end. Big G, thank
you for being my guest.

Big G   Thank *you*, Theo.

Logian   And to all of you: thanks for watching; see you
next week, eleven o'clock, on the dot, *On the
Spot*. Goodnight.

A Matter of Faith

Logian Good evening, and welcome to *On the Spot* as we continue our unique in-depth interviews with God, or Big G, as he prefers to be known. In our first interview, Big G gave us some helpful insights into his way of working. I hope I sum it up fairly if I say that he chooses to work by relationships of love, rather than by control, and to accept the suffering which that inevitably causes him. As part of that, he's fully open to whatever questions, doubts and challenges we might choose to present to him, and so he's here again for another round of them. Welcome to the show, Big G.

Big G Thank you, Theo. Again, it's my pleasure to be here. That's a good summary you gave just now.

Logian I'm glad, because I have to begin by telling you we've taken a lot of flak since last week's show.

Big G I know, Theo, but don't be too despondent. True, there were some critics who didn't take it very seriously –

Logian About as seriously as sugar mines in Siberia, I should say. And it was most of them.

Big G So what are you driving at, Theo?

Logian Well, last week you appeared on world-wide television for the very first time, and –

Big G Oh dear, did it show? I really thought I did rather well for a beginner.

Logian	Yes, you did, actually. Something tells me you've been in the communications business before! No, it's just that as far as I know there's not been a single conversion since last week.
Big G	Oh, I think there were. And Harlequins managed a couple of terrific drop goals in the second half. Did you see it?
Logian	I didn't think you were a sports fan, Big G.
Big G	I'm an admirer of excellence in any healthy field of activity – including rugby fields.
Logian	Tigers* were robbed!
Big G	You may be right. But don't lose hope, Theo. I'm sorry, I've wandered off the point, haven't I. So, you were disappointed that last week's show didn't prove I exist?
Logian	Well, shouldn't it have? It seems to me you had a unique opportunity and let it pass.
Big G	I know it seems rather a letdown, Theo, but it's going to take more than half an hour on late night television to convince people. Some folk wouldn't recognise me in thirty years – not if I hung on a cross right in front of them.
Logian	Ah, but that was different.
Big G	Not a lot. That's the problem with concepts like 'proof' where the supernatural is concerned. I'm afraid I'm unprovable.
Logian	Except of course that you're here, in the flesh,

* Or substitute another local team if you must!

being watched by thirty million viewers worldwide.

Big G   Only thirty million? Well, I suppose it's to be expected when they schedule my slot to clash with *The Good Sex Guide*.

Logian   Whatever the figures are, the point is that you're here, we can all see you, and that must mean something, surely?

Big G   That's right. But the question is: what does it mean? You're a man of faith, Theo, and I've always appreciated that. But you're also a thinker, so you'll know there are other possible interpretations. How do you know this isn't part of some great set-up engineered by the crew to have you on?

Logian   They wouldn't dare. Would they?

Big G   All I'm saying is that there's no such thing as proof. I want to have free and open relationships with people of faith – as I have with you.

Logian   Thank you. But how would proof affect that?

Big G   You wouldn't be free any more. Everyone would *have* to believe in me. And because I'm Big G – God – The Almighty – they'd be coerced into certain ways of living, not out of love but out of fear. No one wants that, or no one in their right mind, anyway.

Logian   Yes, I see the point. But what about Paley's watch?

Big G   Has he lost it?

Logian	Come on, Big G, don't wind me up!
Big G	What are you, Theo, a clock or a garden hose? No, sorry, I couldn't resist it.
Logian	Well if you can't resist temptation what hope is there for us?
Big G	Touché, Theo. Now, what were you asking about Paley's watch?
Logian	Paley said that if there's a watch there must be a watchmaker.
Big G	Yes, and in fact he also said that even if the watch is broken there *still* must have been a watchmaker.
Logian	That's right. He did. It seems to me you're actually making my point for me.
Big G	But what's never been very clear is just what that has to do with proving I exist.
Logian	Well, if the world's a watch . . .
Big G	Then it suggests that I'm the watchmaker, but it isn't so it doesn't and I'm not.
Logian	Can you run that past me again?
Big G	I take it you're wearing a watch, Theo?
Logian	Yes.
Big G	Can you describe it? Without advertising of course, or you'll really get me into trouble.
Logian	I think so. It's got a gold case, leather strap,

	analogue face and a Swiss quartz movement.
Big G	Fine. Now describe the person who made it.
Logian	I'm sorry?
Big G	Well, it's your theory, Theo, not mine. You've got the watch – now describe the watchmaker.
Logian	With all possible respect –
Big G	(– as you said to the Chancellor of the Exchequer last month)
Logian	Whoops! But I meant it, this time.
Big G	I know you did, Theo. Don't worry. What were you going on to say?
Logian	Only that I never said the watch would tell me anything *about* the watchmaker; only that there must *be* one.
Big G	Point taken, Theo. I stand corrected. So your wristwatch, with its gold case, leather strap, analogue face and Swiss movement tells you nothing about the watchmaker?
Logian	No. Except that he's obviously a very good watchmaker.
Big G	Okay, so someone made the watch. I'm quite happy to agree with that. Is he or she still alive?
Logian	I don't know.
Big G	And you can't tell me anything about the maker's personality?

Logian   No.

Big G   So, assuming the world's a watch, what does it tell you about me? And how does it help you to know me?

Logian   I suppose it doesn't. But as you said yourself, the world isn't a watch.

Big G   Good thing, really. Watches are so, well, *mechanical*, aren't they? Don't get me wrong, I like machines, and I appreciate good design. But you can't really have a watch for a friend.

Logian   Which is what you want the world to be to you?

Big G   First and foremost, it's what *I* want to be to the *world*: its friend, rather than its designer. But yes, of course I want it to be a two-way thing – any good relationship is.

Logian   So I suppose that's another reason why there has to be an element of mystery, really – that's a vital element of any friendship.

Big G   Absolutely. Don't you think it's a shame how people think that just because I'm omniscient I don't appreciate mystery? That's all part of the paradox, you might say.

Logian   So faith is about exploration, about mutual trust and so on? Not proof. Of course! You're absolutely right!

Big G   Thank you, Theo. I wish a lot more people would say that to me occasionally. So let's think further, because you've raised an important issue.

Logian   I have?

Big G   Forgive me for saying this, Theo, but perhaps there's an important question you haven't thought of.

Logian   I hardly think so, Big G.

Big G   Don't look so worried – *I* won't tell the producer if *you* don't.

Logian   Oh good. Just keep it between ourselves and the thirty million viewers!

Big G   Absolutely! Now, perhaps it's worth asking *why* people are so desperate to prove I exist.

Logian   Of course, but I knew I could trust you to get to it.

Big G   My word, Theo, you're really making me feel good about myself. I know some people who could use you as a therapist if you ever fancy a change of career.

Logian   Yes, well right now I'm paid to be an interviewer. So what about my question?

Big G   Well done. Never allow your subject to change the subject.

Logian   So, why is it so important to some people to prove you exist?

Big G   I hope you won't mind if I answer with a question –

Logian	I'm getting used to it.
Big G	Good. So, would you like to know that your friends could be relied upon?
Logian	I do know. Well, some of them, anyway.
Big G	*How* do you know?
Logian	Because they've always been there for me in the past.
Big G	And that proves it? Beyond any shadow of doubt?
Logian	Yes.
Big G	Well, you've got some terrific friends, Theo, and as it happens you're right to trust them. But from a purely theoretical point of view I think you might be on shaky ground if you're saying that just because something has been the case in the past you can rely on it for the future. There were times in their history that the Jews thought that about their temples.
Logian	You're not suggesting I can't trust my friends?
Big G	Quite the contrary; I'm saying you've *got* to trust them because it's trust, not knowledge or certainty, that's the basis of any good relationship.
Logian	Can you elaborate a bit?
Big G	Certainly. Take your gas central heating. Dangerous stuff, gas. Don't you worry about waking up with rigor mortis one day?

Logian Well, I get it checked properly every year, and I'm always alert to any smells of gas.

Big G Has the system ever let you down?

Logian No.

Big G So according to what you said about your friends, you should trust it never to fail you in the future. So why have it checked?

Logian Well, it's not quite the same, is it? Gas appliances are a different kettle of fish from people.

Big G Not quite the metaphor I'd have used, but go on; what is the difference between your friends and a gas boiler?

Logian Now, let's see: volatile, full of hot air . . . you know, I'm not sure there *is* any difference.

Big G Oh boy, you're going to be popular for that one!

Logian It'll cost me a round or two I expect, but it's worth it. Seriously, though, the boiler's an object, Big G. A *thing*. It hasn't got a soul. (A *temperament*, perhaps, but not a soul.)

Big G True, but your friends have, haven't they? Souls that is, not temperaments.

Logian Some of them have those, too. But I'm not sure the viewers will all have kept up with you, Big G. Could you explain a little more – just for their benefit, you understand?

Big G That's a good line, Theo, but I wouldn't use it

too often if I were you. All I'm getting at is this. What sort of relationship would you have with your family and friends if you kept asking for evidence to prove you could trust them?

Logian   A dreadful one – which is precisely why I wouldn't do that.

Big G   No, but quite a lot of people seem to be rather less fussy where I'm concerned.

Logian   That must infuriate you.

Big G   No, it saddens me – really saddens me. But I understand why they do it. People like certainty; in an uncertain world there's nothing strange about that. The trouble is that they miss out on so much, and I think it's a shame.

Logian   Why's it a shame?

Big G   Well, because as you've indicated, certainty isn't there to be had. If you wait until you're certain before you trust somebody then the friendship never even gets off the ground because people will always be unpredictable; that's part of being human.

Logian   I suppose you could have made us differently.

Big G   Yes, and then Paley's analogy would have been right. You'd have been machines, not humans, and incapable of relationships anyway, which defeats the whole point.

Logian   So you're saying that it's faith, not knowledge, that makes for good relationships?

Big G   That's not a bad summary, although like all summaries it's rather over-simplified.

Logian   Exactly. That was my next point. There's more to it than that, isn't there? I mean, if it were that simple, we could believe in anything, couldn't we?

Big G   Go on?

Logian   Well you're right, of course, in what you say, but it's still true that my faith in my friends has *something* to do with what I know about them: how reliable they've been in the past, and so on. Isn't that true?

Big G   Absolutely, and where does that lead you, Theo?

Logian   So believing in you, and trusting you, must be based on some kind of experience – some degree of knowledge – or we might just as well believe in fairies. Which I don't of course. Or not in the last year or two anyway.

Big G   You're right about needing knowledge as well as faith, but they're not the same thing, are they? Faith interprets knowledge.

Logian   In what way?

Big G   Pour me some water, would you? . . . That's enough, thank you.

Logian   The glass is only half full.

Big G   Yes, but it is half *full*. Not half *empty*.

Logian   Isn't it both?

Big G   Could be, but not necessarily. That's a matter of faith. Let's take another example. What's likely to be in the news tomorrow?

Logian   Oh, don't talk to me about news! Have you noticed it's all bad these days? Murders, famines, wars, marriage break-ups . . .

Big G   Do you really think it's *all* bad, Theo? Every day, I see the most wonderful little acts of kindness, self-sacrifice, even heroism, by ordinary people who'll never get a mention in the papers. Right now, as we speak, babies are being born who are wanted and will be loved. Somewhere, an off-duty nurse is going into a ward to sit with a dying patient because she wants to, not because she's paid to. An ambitious and successful young man is turning down promotion to spend more time with his family. There are so many of these things I could tell you about, who'd ever be a cynic?

Logian   So it's not such a bad old world, after all!

Big G   Take my word, Theo. No, actually, *don't* take my word – take a look around.

Logian   Is faith like beauty, then – in the eye of the beholder?

Big G   Yes, to some extent. Some people look at the world and see only darkness; others the light that shines in it. It's a bit like those clever pictures you can get: some see a vase, others see two faces.

Logian   So it all comes down to individual points of view? One belief is as good as another?

Big G	I thought that was where you were leading! Let me paint you a picture, Theo. You're in a lonely place, and it's very dark. All around you a storm is raging: rain lashing down, wind threatening to blow you off your feet. Not very positive, is it?
Logian	Not very.
Big G	Fine. Now you notice something strange: a light – a candle, to be exact – burning right in the middle of the storm. Not very brightly, but definitely still alight. What's your question?
Logian	What, staying alight in all the wind and rain?
Big G	That's right.
Logian	*How's* it staying alight?
Big G	*That's* your question!
Logian	What's the answer?
Big G	That's where faith comes in – and faith is much more about questions than about answers. The point is, Theo, you've got a choice. You can focus your attention on the negative things – which seem pretty overwhelming – and say there are no grounds for belief, or you can find the one tiny glimmer of hope and ask what keeps it alive. That's faith.
Logian	But why don't you just get rid of the darkness altogether – make all the evil go away?
Big G	Oh, that'll happen, Theo, don't worry. And if I were an engineer I'd do it straight away. But

we're back to relationships. Wherever I can do it by love, not by force, I *am* getting rid of the darkness. But I'm not going to do it any other way; it would be against my nature.

Logian   And meanwhile we all suffer?

Big G   No one more than me; that's the cost of love. And love that's willing to suffer is the most powerful force around.

Logian   That seems a good point on which to end. Big G, thank you very much indeed. And to all of you, thanks for watching. See you next week: eleven o'clock, on the dot, *On the Spot*. Goodnight.

A Plug for the Book

Logian   Good evening and welcome again to *On the Spot* in this very special series of interviews. We often have guests appearing on this show with the intention of getting a plug for some book they've written in the hope that it might thereby become a best seller. Tonight it's different. The book is *already* a best seller, and has been since any of us can remember. Some describe it as the greatest literature in the world; others claim that it's riddled with inconsistencies; secular feminists denounce it as patriarchalist propaganda, and more blood has been shed over it than any other document. The book is the Bible, and here to talk about it is its author. Welcome, Big G.

Big G   Thank you. Good evening.

Logian   Let's get the basic argument cleared up straight away. Did you write this book, and is it true?

Big G   Well, I really would like to help, but I think you'll find that it's not *quite* as simple as that, Theo.

Logian   I'd have thought it was *absolutely* that simple. Either you wrote it or you didn't; either it's true or it's not. What could be simpler?

Big G   It's a bit like the proverbial 'Have you stopped beating your wife?' question. A straight yes or no doesn't really do it justice.

Logian   But surely, that's a deliberate catch question. I asked you a totally straightforward one. Did you write the Bible?

Big G   Do you mean, did I actually hold a pen in my hand and create the text letter by letter?

Logian   Well, no. Of course I didn't mean it *that* literally. Okay, you've made your point. I'll accept that that part of the question is open to interpretation. But what about the second half? It's either true or it's not.

Big G   Would you mind if we stay with the first half for a little longer, Theo?

Logian   You wouldn't be avoiding the issue, by any chance?

Big G   Oh, no – not in the least; we seem to have got a bit hung up on the wording. Look, will it help if I say that the Bible was inspired by me?

Logian   I thought that was what I asked.

Big G   Not quite, you asked whether I *wrote* the Bible.

Logian   But it comes to the same thing in this instance.

Big G   Let me put it this way. To say that I *wrote* the Bible is a little like saying you wrote that short story for Dan – the one that won him a school prize.

Logian   I did *not* write it! It was all his own work. I never thought I'd say this to you, Big G, but you should be careful what you say. People might misunderstand.

Big G   Right! Now you see what I'm driving at? You didn't write that story, of course, but you *did* inspire it.

Logian   Did I?

Big G   It was about a child who longed to be a journalist, and then grew up and found out that it isn't all it's cracked up to be.

Logian   You're right. I'd never realised before.

Big G   So you're happy to say you inspired it?

Logian   Now you point it out, yes.

Big G   But not that you wrote it?

Logian   No. And not just because of the split infinitive in the final paragraph.

Big G   Why, then?

Logian   Because I don't want to detract from his achievement. I'm really glad to have had a part in it, though.

Big G   So you won't mind, then, if I say that I inspired the Bible, but didn't actually write it?

Logian   I can see the distinction you're trying to make, Big G, but it's still rather unclear. I mean, just *how* did you inspire it?

Big G   How did you inspire Dan?

Logian   I didn't know I was, to be honest.

Big G   That's interesting. So you didn't wake up one morning and think, 'I'm going to inspire Dan to write a prize-winning story about a disillusioned journalist'?

Logian	Heavens, no! Sorry, Big G.
Big G	Don't worry, Theo. My good friend Paul used a similar kind of phrase in his letters to the churches, but pious translators watered it down to 'by no means' – I ask you! So how did Dan's inspiration come about?
Logian	I suppose it must have been happening when we were talking together.
Big G	Or, perhaps, playing together?
Logian	Yes, maybe.
Big G	We're really very alike, you and I, which I suppose shouldn't be surprising. So the inspiration happened in your ordinary relationship. You and Dan have talked together, played together, laughed and cried together – I always enjoy your games, you know – and then what he actually wrote was *inspired* by you but *written* by him.
Logian	I see what you're driving at. But it doesn't quite work. I didn't interfere with Dan's writing, but I would have done if I'd had to.
Big G	Go on?
Logian	Well, some of the biblical writers have said some things that I'd *definitely* have censored if I'd been you.
Big G	But you're not me.
Logian	No, but don't say it too loudly. My secretary might hear you.

Big G   Fair enough, Theo. Can you give me some examples?

Logian   There's an awful lot of blood lust in the Bible; and most of the time people ascribe it to you. Did you really tell your people to do such horrible things to their enemies?

Big G   What do you think, Theo?

Logian   If you did, you'll be getting no more 'alleluias' or 'praise his names' from me, for a start.

Big G   Well said. It's bad enough that people do these horrible things to each other, but when they convince themselves that I approve of it . . . and then for people to believe them . . .

Logian   I don't *want* to, Big G, but if those passages are wrong why are they there?

Big G   Partly for the same reason that the split infinitive's still in Dan's story. Because it's inspired, not dictated. But tell me what you learn from those parts of Scripture.

Logian   I don't want to upset you, Big G, but to be candid I've never got anything at all from passages like that.

Big G   Bless you, Theo, I'm not *that* sensitive! It's how people treat each other, not the Bible, that gets to me. Let me put it another way. What does all that violence and ghastliness tell you *about the writer*?

Logian   Seems to me he was sanctifying his own desires by attributing them to you.

Big G   It's not at all uncommon, I'm afraid. People do it all the time, and things were no different in biblical days.

Logian   And now?

Big G   It's not so long since the Dutch Reformed Church in South Africa were claiming that I approved of Apartheid. Now that *really* got to me, but I danced in the streets when they corrected it!

Logian   So the kind of biblical verses I've been querying should have been a warning to them. But what have they got to say to ordinary people like you and – whoops – like me?

Big G   You know, Theo, I rather liked that. 'Ordinary'. Most people put me on a pedestal and then complain they can't relate to me! Anyway, to address your question: I do remember an instance of someone who thought I wanted him to have a bigger house. Before I could get through to him to deny it, he'd got it all worked out. He needed a bigger study so that he could work for me better, and a larger lounge and garden so he could hold functions for the church, and so it went on. Before long, he'd convinced himself that he was really doing it for me.

Logian   I don't mind people knowing that was me, Big G. And you're right – I really did convince myself I was doing it all for you.

Big G   Of course you did, Theo, and you're very far from alone. So perhaps there is something you can learn from those passages, after all.

Logian	So you're saying that the biblical writers can speak to us in ways they themselves didn't even realise?
Big G	Close. I'm saying that *I* can speak through the things they write. I love working *with* people – not against them. And however wrong they get things, I can always bring something good out of it, even if it's not what ideally I'd have wanted.
Logian	Of course! Redemption.
Big G	Exactly! The most rewarding part of my work: taking what is apparently lost and turning it to good.
Logian	We seem to have moved on to the second part of my question: about whether the Bible's true or not. I realise now that it isn't.
Big G	When did I say that?
Logian	Earlier on, I asked whether the Bible was true.
Big G	And I haven't answered that, yet.
Logian	But everything you've just said –
Big G	– suggests that there are parts that aren't *factual*.
Logian	That's right.
Big G	Not that it's not *true*.
Logian	But everyone knows that all facts are true. That's the definition.
Big G	Absolutely, Theo. No question about it. But is all truth factual?

Logian   You sound like a lawyer.

Big G   Some people think I am, but I find grace much more exciting.

Logian   Grace who?

Big G   Now you're trying to wind *me* up, Theo!

Logian   What are you, Big G, a gramophone or a public company?

Big G   Boy, I walked into that one, didn't I! Now, this thing about truth and fact: I take it you've heard the story of the boy who cried wolf?

Logian   Of course. I was telling it to Luke, my youngest, the other day.

Big G   I know, I was eavesdropping at the time. But tell me: is it a factual story?

Logian   I haven't the faintest idea, but does it matter?

Big G   Not in the least – except presumably to the people involved – but it does contain *truth*, doesn't it?

Logian   Right. So it doesn't matter whether the Bible is factual or not, so long as we grasp its truths?

Big G   I wouldn't go quite so far as that, Theo, but you're on the right lines.

Logian   So those people who say the Bible's history are off their –

Big G   Off beam is the word you're looking for, I think, Theo. Not as far off as you're suggesting. The Bible *is* history.

Logian   But you just said it wasn't factual.

Big G   To be quite precise, I said it wasn't necessary for it to be factual in order for it to be true. That doesn't mean it's complete fiction.

Logian   So some parts are history and some aren't?

Big G   You're missing the point, Theo.

Logian   Well, perhaps it would be more helpful if you were to clarify the point for me, Big G?

Big G   Certainly. I imagine that when you were at school you were taught in History that Columbus discovered the New World.

Logian   Yes, I was.

Big G   Except that it wasn't 'new' at all, was it?

Logian   I suppose it *existed* before, but no one knew about it. So it was new in that sense.

Big G   *No one* knew about it?

Logian   Well, I suppose the natives did.

Big G   So someone *did* know about it before Columbus invaded it?

Logian   Invaded?

Big G   Just another word, Theo, but one which would seem more appropriate if you were a native of the Americas.

Logian   I'd never heard it used that way before.

Big G   So, then, who is right? Was it discovery or invasion?

Logian   I suppose it depends on your point of view. But what's this got to do with the Bible?

Big G   Nothing much, except to show that it can be history without being factual. All history is interpretation, as you've just demonstrated. Especially the history of any relationship.

Logian   Go on.

Big G   If I ask you about your personal history, you could talk in objective, factual statements: when you were born, what schools you attended, and so on. But if you start talking about your relationship with me – or with anyone else for that matter – then all you can really do is give your side of it. And that's very subjective.

Logian   Of course it is, but that doesn't mean it's any less valuable.

Big G   Absolutely. So now we're agreed that statements don't need to be factual to be truthful, and history can be of value even when it isn't strictly objective or accurate. If nothing else, it gives insights into human nature

Logian   So it seems that we need to treat the Bible with a good deal of caution.

Big G   You need to treat the Bible with a good deal of *respect* and you don't do that by reading it like a kind of users' manual for the world.

Logian   So how *should* we read it?

Big G   D'you remember how we set up these interviews, Theo?

Logian   Do I just! During the negotiations, you accused me of being deferential. I've been called some things in my time but nobody's ever called me *that* before.

Big G   So treat the Bible with the same kind of respect you have me – get into a dialogue with it. Challenge it, probe it, get under its skin. And don't let it get away with anything that doesn't ring true.

Logian   Because it might not be.

Big G   Because it might not be *factual*. You might have to make a little more of an effort before you understand it properly.

Logian   Yes, of course. Well, Big G, it's a pity we can't continue this interview for longer, but time, tide and the late-night movie wait for no man.

Big G   Or God.

Logian   Big G, thank you very much for being my guest again.

Big G   Thank *you*, Theo. And if ever I *do* write a book, I promise I'll give you the first interview about it.

Logian   We'll look forward to it. Meanwhile, thanks for watching. See you next week, eleven o'clock, on the dot, *On the Spot*. Goodnight.

G is for Gender

Logian	Good evening and welcome again to *On the Spot* – the show where anything can happen and most things do. We continue our exclusive series of interviews, and with me once again is the most surprising and unnerving but also by far the most exciting guest it has been my privilege to interview – or perhaps, in this case, be interviewed by, which is what usually seems to happen. When we devised and named this show the idea was that the interviewer would put the guest 'on the spot', but in recent weeks the boot has very definitely been on the other foot. Big G, I hope you won't mind if I express some surprise at your appearance.
Big G	I'm sorry, Theo. Don't you like it?
Logian	Well, you're undoubtedly radically different tonight from the way you've looked during our previous interviews.
Big G	I expect it's the dress.
Logian	It's certainly *related* to that.
Big G	I'd hoped you'd like it, Theo: simple but elegant is how I would describe it – don't you agree?
Logian	Oh, the dress is fine. It's just that I'd never thought of you as a woman.
Big G	And you're right, of course, Theo, because I'm not.
Logian	Well you're certainly not a man. Unless of course . . .

Big G   Right again, Theo. I'm not a man. And I'm not a woman, either, but it would seem strange if I weren't equally able to take that form, wouldn't it? You're known for having a positive attitude to women's issues, aren't you?

Logian   I'd certainly like to think so.

Big G   So where do you think all those good feminine qualities come from?

Logian   Ah, now that's a different question. To say that feminine qualities come from God is one thing, but that doesn't mean we have to say God's a woman.

Big G   Absolutely right. Now try saying that about masculine qualities.

Logian   I'm not with you.

Big G   Well, presumably you would also argue that saying that masculine qualities come from God is one thing, but that doesn't mean we have to say God's a man.

Logian   This is fascinating! But surely, you're always male in Scripture.

Big G   You're right that most of the time I'm portrayed in masculine terms (I don't think that's quite the same as 'male', actually) but of course you know those passages about bringing creation to birth? According to Isaiah, I'm like a woman in labour.* And let me tell you that compared with being the creator of all this, childbirth's a doddle.

* Isaiah 42:14

Logian	'Childbirth.' Now that's a very interesting idea. It puts quite a different complexion on the problem of pain, doesn't it?
Big G	Go on, Theo, I think you're onto something.
Logian	Jesus said something about birth-pains, didn't he?
Big G	The birth-pains of the kingdom, yes. Well done, Theo. So –
Logian	So creation is an on-going process in which the pain is shared between creation and creator?
Big G	I like it, Theo, just as long as the pain is still taken seriously. Just because there's hope, it doesn't take the agony away.
Logian	Of course. But however exciting this idea may be, I've often criticised other people for building whole concepts on a single verse or reference from the Bible, and I don't want to be accused of that myself.
Big G	Quite right, too, but this isn't the only reference, is it? Doesn't Paul say something very similar in Romans 8?
Logian	The bit about all creation groaning in childbirth. Of course! This gets better all the time! Then I suppose there's the Wisdom literature – all that stuff about your wisdom being feminine.
Big G	Yes, I must say I rather liked that. Wisdom is feminine: now there's something for people who think women are irrational to chew on.

Logian	Mind you, it's still only a very small part of the Bible, and for the rest of the time it overwhelmingly uses masculine images. You can hardly blame people for thinking they're the ones that matter.
Big G	Of course not, and I'm not *blaming* anybody. But you could argue it the other way round: that for feminine images to have survived at all against those odds means they ought to be taken seriously.
Logian	Well, they'll have to be now, won't they?
Big G	I doubt it. As we've observed before, people will believe what they want to believe, and I'm prepared to lay bets on the number of letters you'll get next week accusing you of indulging in cheap, politically correct stunts.
Logian	I think you'd have an unfair advantage there. Anyway, you don't approve of gambling, do you?
Big G	A figure of speech, Theo. Nothing more.
Logian	So you're quite happy to be thought of as feminine as well as masculine?
Big G	I'd prefer not to be limited to either, but then I end up getting called 'it' which I really think leaves a lot to be desired.
Logian	Does it really matter whether people think of you in masculine or feminine terms? Surely, it's who you are that matters?
Big G	Absolutely. But as long as people think I'm a

male they can go on from there to think that men were made more in my image than women.

Logian   If I may say so, they'd find it hard to think that at the moment.

Big G   Is there something on your mind, Theo? Other than my femininity, that is?

Logian   It's difficult to express but, since you ask: I can now understand why you chose to appear on the show as a woman, but couldn't you have been a rather less beautiful woman?

Big G   All people are beautiful, Theo. Male, female, old, young – if you're asking me to be human and not beautiful you're asking the impossible.

Logian   Come on, Big G; I think you know what I mean.

Big G   You find it hard to relate to me as Big G when I look like this?

Logian   Frankly, yes.

Big G   But you have no problem with those traditional tall-dark-and-handsome pictures of Jesus?

Logian   Somehow, it's not the same.

Big G   No, of course not. People are used to seeing me portrayed as a very attractive *man*, but not as an attractive *woman*.

Logian   So you don't think that there's anything wrong with looking the way you do at the moment?

Big G   I could find that question offensive, Theo. Would I look like this, if I thought it was wrong?

Logian   Come on, Big G. You know what I mean. Some people might say you were –

Big G   *[Interrupting Theo]* It's a funny thing, isn't it, Theo – how men are 'snappily dressed' and women are 'tarted up'.

Logian   Be fair, Big G; I didn't use that expression.

Big G   No. And *you* wouldn't, but you're not everybody.

Logian   Point taken, Big G, but if you're as pro-women as you seem to be, why weren't there any among Jesus' disciples?

Big G   I don't think I follow you, Theo.

Logian   It's a simple enough question. The whole of the New Testament is dominated by men.

Big G   You're absolutely right in saying that men tend to take the thing over, but that's not by any design on my part. And I think you mean women *apostles*, actually. If you read the story as Luke tells it you'll find the women *disciples* were very important. They actually provided for Jesus, financially.

Logian   So he was a kept man, then?

Big G   Yes, I suppose he was. What a delightful idea!

Logian   But the men got all the plum parts, though, didn't they?

Big G　　　Oh, they hogged a great deal of the limelight, yes. But then, what about men like Joseph, and Zechariah? It was Mary and Elizabeth that got the big parts there; the men were just in supporting roles. And actually, they got pushed well out of the picture.

Logian　　　Yes, but they're the exceptions that prove the rule. You've got to admit that all the important events are dominated by men.

Big G　　　'Dominated' is a very masculine kind of word, Theo, but there are other ways of being important. Look at the crucifixion stories: how many of the men disciples were present there?

Logian　　　Well, I think –

Big G　　　Most of them ran away in the garden, at the arrest, and Peter stayed for a while but wished he hadn't. It was the women who were there at the big moments, not the men.

Logian　　　Yes, I grant you that, but they still don't get much of a profile, just standing there.

Big G　　　Don't knock just standing there, Theo. Sometimes it's all there is to do. And it's a sight more worthwhile than doing nothing. Can you remember interviewing the Foreign Secretary some years ago during the war in Beirut?

Logian　　　The siege of the refugee camps. Yes, I remember. We actually got some action on that one, too; I was quite pleased about it.

Big G　　　You did very well with it. But can you

	remember what it was that really turned the interview?
Logian	Wasn't it then that we'd heard of a British woman doctor and nurse who were trapped in the camps?
Big G	Yes. Except that they weren't merely trapped. They'd *chosen* to stay there.
Logian	They were really special, those two.
Big G	A pair of vulnerable women, taking the risk of standing with crucified people. Hardly an insignificant part to play, was it?
Logian	Of course! I see what you mean.
Big G	It's those who stay through the night that witness the dawn.
Logian	Yes. A bit of a cliché, if I might say so, Big G, but an appropriate one.
Big G	Thank you, Theo.
Logian	But that doesn't get you off the hook, though, does it? They might have witnessed the resurrection, but the men ran the church, and still do.
Big G	There's a lot in that, Theo, but you really have got to get away from this idea that just because things happen a certain way, that's what I wanted. It was the women who were sent to tell the story. Think about it for a moment. They met Jesus, after the resurrection, and were sent to proclaim the news to others. What does that make them?

Logian	Pretty excited, I should think.
Big G	Be serious, Theo – live up to your name for a minute. What would a *theologian* say that made them?
Logian	Apostles! The women were apostles! Corks! That's one in the eye for the –
Big G	Quite, Theo. But when it comes to sexism in the Church, no one's entirely innocent, even the most radical.
Logian	Well, I'll be a monkey's Godfather!
Big G	Difficult, even for me, Theo. And quite unacceptable to the Church. Well, most of the Church, anyway.
Logian	So why didn't the women get the recognition they deserved?
Big G	I think you'd better put that question to the men who didn't believe them.
Logian	That's a bit difficult, Big G, since they're all dead.
Big G	Well, that's another question. But be that as it may, you might perhaps remember the story of the walk to Emmaus, Theo – how on the way to Emmaus, Cleopas said that no one believed the story the women had told.
Logian	Yes.
Big G	And then, when they got back to Jerusalem afterwards, what were they told? 'It's true

after all, and we believe it because *Simon* says so.' They could believe a man, you see.

Logian   So you're saying the Gospel was hijacked by men?

Big G   Not in those words. It was supposed to be for them, too.

Logian   Very well, but the basic point remains the same. You're saying that the women were the first to proclaim resurrection, the men didn't believe them, and then when they found out that it *was* true, behaved as though they'd found out for themselves?

Big G   All I'm doing, Theo, is pointing out what the Bible itself says. If you want to turn it into a feminist manifesto, that's quite another thing.

Logian   It's not a case of what I want to make it. That's how you're making it sound.

Big G   The gospel of resurrection was given to women, who were told to share it with the men. It wasn't to be their property, any more than it was that of any particular group or race or anything else.

Logian   Oh. So you're *not* a feminist, then?

Big G   I'm not any kind of 'ist'. I'm interested in relationships: healthy relationships in which people can love each other, and themselves as well. And that can't happen in a situation of injustice – whether it's between male and female, black and white, or whatever.

Logian	But *is* it unjust to recognise that people have different roles in society? I mean, didn't you specifically *design* women to be mothers, and doesn't that mean that their first priority should always be their families?
Big G	Of course.
Logian	Ah! So the traditionalists are right, after all!
Big G	There again, on the same basis you could also say that I specifically designed men to be fathers, and *their* first priority should be their families, too.
Logian	That doesn't mean we can't do anything else, though.
Big G	Precisely, Theo. Let's pursue this a little further. Most people have got a perfectly good set of fingers, haven't they?
Logian	Yes.
Big G	So you could say that they're equipped to be typists. There again, most people have a good pair of legs, fundamentally identical to Linford Christie's.
Logian	Ah, but that's my point. Men and women equally have legs, but men and women don't equally have the ability to be pregnant.
Big G	Which means that women are defined solely in terms of that special ability. How would you like me to apply the same argument to men, Theo?
Logian	You can't.

Big G   Never say that to me, Theo. It's not advisable. I think the argument would go something like this. If women are defined totally in terms of their ability to become pregnant, then perhaps men should be defined solely by their capacity to *make* women pregnant. In which case you, having fathered all the children you want to, are now redundant. Superfluous.

Logian   Oh, that's ridiculous!

Big G   Glad you think so, Theo. You see, once you take any single characteristic, whether it's gender, race, colour, sexuality or the circumference of the big toe, and define a person's place in the world by that alone, then it does indeed get ridiculous.

Logian   That wasn't what I was doing.

Big G   No, Theo, you were doing your job as an interviewer – and doing it very well, too. But some people *do* think that way, and they have a lot of influence. You've given me the opportunity to address some of them, and that's great. Thank you very much.

Logian   Thank *you*, Big G. And to all of you, thanks for watching; see you next week: eleven o'clock, on the dot, *On the Spot*. Goodnight.

The 'S' Word

Logian	Good evening and welcome to *On the Spot* as we continue our exclusive series of interviews with God. You may remember that last week I was a little taken aback by the appearance of Big G on this show in the guise of a woman. However, this week, much to my relief, everything's back to normal. Welcome, Big G.
Big G	What was that, Theo?
Logian	I said, 'Welcome, Big G'.
Big G	Thank you very much. But I actually meant what you said just before that. Something about everything being back to normal?
Logian	Oh, yes.
Big G	And what precisely is 'normal', Theo?
Logian	Well, you know.
Big G	No, I'm afraid I don't. Normality is a category of quite human origins; there's nothing divinely ordained about it. And then, of course, it's very subjective. People think that they and their lifestyles are 'normal' and they define 'normality' accordingly. So what's 'normal' for one person isn't for someone else. And that means you can say that nothing's 'normal'.
Logian	And therefore nothing's abnormal, by the same definition – I like it! Seriously, though, it's clever stuff, Big G, but you surely must admit that some things are, let's say, more familiar than others.

Big G   Absolutely right, and you've put your finger on the problem. When something's familiar, people begin to call it normal, and it's only a short step from there –

Logian   – to thinking that it's divinely ordained for all eternity. Yes, it's a good point.

Big G   So it's understandable that, since that's how I'm most often portrayed, people tend to think of it as 'normal' to visualise me as a white, middle class male.

Logian   Yes, I see what you mean, but it's not strictly what we're here for tonight. So without further ado, let's get on with the interview.

Big G   I think that would be an excellent idea, Theo. Now, what did you want to ask me?

Logian   Big G, what do you think about sex?

Big G   Wicked! Absolutely wicked!

Logian   *Wicked?*

Big G   Something wrong, Theo?

Logian   Well, I'm sure that *some* people will be glad you said that, Big G, but I really expected you to say that it was good.

Big G   That's right. Good. Wonderful. Terrific. Wicked.

Logian   Oh, I see. I'm sorry, but I didn't expect you to use slang.

Big G   Language is a living organism. It grows, and

	changes, and you have to grow and change with it.
Logian	That sounds like a very lax attitude, to me. Shouldn't we teach people to use it properly?
Big G	It would make life a lot easier – not to mention biblical scholarship – but we'd lose a lot as well. Anyway, it's not really practical; King Canute proved that, I think.
Logian	But if you just go with the flow, then words can mean anything and you're in constant danger of being misunderstood.
Big G	Well, that happens either way. Can I give you an example?
Logian	Feel free.
Big G	How would you react if I said you were a very indifferent interviewer?
Logian	You may be right, but I wouldn't like you saying it.
Big G	But if I said that you were a strictly *impartial* interviewer – which would be more accurate – you'd take it as a compliment?
Logian	That's quite different.
Big G	It is now, but it's not long since the two were substantially the same. Strictly speaking the word still means what it always did, but no one understands it that way, now.
Logian	Fair enough, I take your point, but it wasn't semantics we were supposed to discuss.

Big G   Of course not. Sorry, Theo, but words are fascinating things. Now, you're about to pull me back into line, I think.

Logian   Sex.

Big G   Wicked! Haven't we been here before?

Logian   But you must have more to say about it than that. I mean, there's a lot of concern about the amount there is on films and television these days.

Big G   Ah, so you're not asking me about sex, are you? You're asking me what I think about excess! Theo, if you'd asked me what I thought about peppermint creams, I'd probably have said they were delicious. If you then ask whether they should be shoved down people's throats in copious portions for several hours a day, I'd have to say it's not a good idea.

Logian   I take the point, but it's not the same, though, is it? I mean, you can't seriously compare the harm done by sex with confectionery. Get real, Big G.

Big G   Of course they're not the same – there's a huge difference. All I was saying was that just because something is overindulged in or misused doesn't mean it's bad.

Logian   Very well. So what is the proper use of sex?

Big G   What would you think about that, Theo?

Logian   Here we go again. Why do you always turn the questions back upon me?

Big G   Why do you think?

Logian   You're doing it again – but I'm not going to rise to it. What was the first question again?

Big G   I was asking you what *you* thought sex was for.

Logian   Strictly speaking, I suppose the procreation of children.

Big G   Oh well, if we're going to be strictly speaking about it . . . what's food for?

Logian   To maintain our bodies.

Big G   Fine, but does it have any other function?

Logian   It's a social thing, I suppose – or antisocial according to how it's done!

Big G   Now we're getting there. Anything else?

Logian   Since you press me on it, I do sometimes eat just for enjoyment.

Big G   Okay. Now tell me why you took up squash.

Logian   To keep fit – and to work off a few of the chocolate bars – but I don't see the connection.

Big G   You will. So, you eat out of necessity, you also do it for social reasons, and sometimes solely for pleasure. Would you say the same about playing squash?

Logian   Yes, I suppose I would.

Big G   Good. So, the fact that something's got a practical purpose doesn't mean it can't also be

	used just for pleasure, as well. So what about sex?
Logian	You can't be serious. 'Let's see, will it be squash or sex this afternoon, or shall we just pop out for a jam doughnut?'
Big G	Now *you're* the one being frivolous, Theo.
Logian	It wasn't me that put sex on a level with food and exercise.
Big G	Now if I did that, you'd be right to object. But all I was doing was making the point that there doesn't have to be one sole purpose to anything.
Logian	So you don't mind if people use sex purely for pleasure?
Big G	That depends on what you call 'pleasure', I suppose; it's not the same as indulgence. And it's not people 'using' *sex* for pleasure that's the problem so much as their 'using' each other.
Logian	And that's where marriage comes in? A lot of people now think it's an outmoded institution.
Big G	Well if it's become an institution in the first place, then perhaps it should be outmoded. The best thing that can happen to institutions is that they become redundant.
Logian	An awful lot of people are going to hear that as anti-marriage.
Big G	Far from it; I love marriage – and far too much to be happy about its becoming an institution.

Logian Sorry, Big G. Wrong choice of words.

Big G No, Theo, don't apologise – it was precisely the right choice of words. All too often, marriage *is* an institution; and what it ought to be is a relationship.

Logian Right. Marriage *is* the right context for sex, then. So what about living in sin?

Big G Well, I'd rather people didn't do it, but everyone does of course.

Logian Everyone?

Big G Without exception.

Logian Well, *I* never did.

Big G Really? Oh, I see. You're talking about living tally – living over the brush – married but not churched – whatever phrase people care to use. I thought you meant sin.

Logian Same thing, isn't it?

Big G Well, sex *can* be sinful, but not all sin is sexual, is it? Everybody sins, and some do worse things than having sex outside marriage. Hence, everybody lives 'in sin'.

Logian Very well, Big G, let me rephrase it. What about sex outside marriage?

Big G It's a good question, and I'm not going to ignore it, but would you mind answering one for me?

Logian Go on.

Big G   What about abusive relationships within marriage?

Logian   Somehow I get the idea you're trying to avoid the issue.

Big G   No pun intended, I presume, Theo? On the contrary, I'm trying to get *to* the issue. Let's take a hypothetical case: a couple are legally married, but the spark's gone. They don't converse, they don't pay each other very much attention, because to be honest they don't like each other very much; the only reason they're still together is inertia. But from time to time when one or both of them feel the need they make the sprung base – if not actually the earth – move. It's all quite respectable, of course, because they're 'married'. Next door live a young couple who haven't got married because they've known too many people like their neighbours and got a bit cynical about it. But they love each other, they've got real commitment and when they make love it's an act of mutual self-giving. Of course, they have to put up with disapproving gossip, because they're 'not married'. Now, you tell me: who's having healthy sex?

Logian   So sex outside marriage is okay, then?

Big G   That wasn't what I said. I was challenging the suggestion that a public ceremony and a legal document constitute a marriage.

Logian   Oh, I'm with you. So we don't need to get legally married: the ceremony's redundant, as long as we really love one another and stay faithful.

Big G   Saints alive, Theo! Where d'you get all these words you keep putting into my mouth?

Logian   Well, I thought they came from you actually.

Big G   Don't worry, you're not the first person to make that mistake. What I'm saying is not that people shouldn't marry, but that marriage is *first and foremost* a relationship – not a contract or a social institution. And it's the quality of the relationship, not the legal niceties, that makes good sex out of what would otherwise be fornication.

Logian   But presumably we could have the relationship without the ceremony and the legalities. Would that still be marriage? A lot of cohabiting couples claim that what they've got is as good.

Big G   Would a Rembrandt still be a Rembrandt if it weren't in a frame, Theo?

Logian   I suppose so. Not that I find Rembrandt particularly sexy. Reubens, now – that's quite another thing.

Big G   Okay. So why put a Rembrandt – I think we'd better stick with him for the sake of maintaining concentration – why put a Rembrandt in a frame if it's just as good without one?

Logian   Now who's putting words into whose mouth? I never said it was just as good, merely that it would still be a Rembrandt.

Big G   Ah! Now you've hit it. So the frame has a value, after all.

Logian	Yes, it defines the work, contains it. And it sets it off very nicely, as well.
Big G	So why not just have the frame?
Logian	You know, I could have sworn we were talking about marriage.
Big G	Well, go on: *you* make the connections (if you'll forgive me for making you sound like a railway timetable).
Logian	So . . . we need both.
Big G	Right, Theo. You need the content *and* the context: the relationship *and* the social framework. But when all's said and done it's the *content* that matters. Although it *can* stand without the frame, it's infinitely better with it. But the frame with no content is redundant.
Logian	It's a nice theory, Big G, but I'm beginning to wonder whether the social framework's necessary at all, on this basis.
Big G	People need structures, Theo, especially if they're going to be as open and as vulnerable as a good marriage requires. But the point remains that it's the relationship that counts.
Logian	And if the relationship breaks down?
Big G	Pretty well all relationships break down to one extent or another at some point; it's a question of whether or not they're repairable.
Logian	You make marriage sound like a motor car.

Big G	There could be worse comparisons, I suppose.
Logian	Now this I've got to hear.
Big G	Well, you could say that they start off all shiny and new, with great excitement and pride; for a while they get cared for and properly maintained –
Logian	Then they get neglected and taken for granted, and start to go wrong.
Big G	You really are an old cynic, Theo. Worrying in one so young! That doesn't *need* to happen. Some people carry on taking a pride in their cars and looking after them, and they last a lifetime.
Logian	Some people give more care to their cars than their marriages.
Big G	Unfortunately true, but let's stick with the analogy for now. What do old cars eventually become?
Logian	Spare parts for other old cars?
Big G	I suppose I asked for that. I was really thinking in terms of classics.
Logian	Why, what did Plato ever say about cars?
Big G	Not those classics, Theo. Classic *cars*.
Logian	Oh! And I suppose you're going to say that well-maintained marriages become classics, too?
Big G	In a sense. They're treasured – valued. All the

	years of tender loving care give them a special kind of shine that nothing straight off the altar can ever have.
Logian	So you're going to tell me that sex is a kind of marital routine maintenance?
Big G	Heavens, no! But it's part of the marriage, and the way it's used can make it or break it. We got into this by talking about breakdowns. If a marriage is breaking down, nipping between the sheets for two minutes –
Logian	*Two minutes?!*
Big G	Don't believe all you read, Theo. Anyway, two minutes or two hours, it's not going to mend a broken marriage.
Logian	OK. So marriage is really about a relationship, not a contract. Sex is important, but not the be all and end all, and the relationship needs to be worked at and is *worth* working at. But what I'm getting at is, why get married? If it's the relationship that counts why not just have that? I mean, to return to the analogy you used a few minutes ago, a Reubens is still a Rembrandt if it hasn't got a frame.
Big G	You've got a real problem there, haven't you, Theo?
Logian	You could be right. Still, you know what I meant.
Big G	Yes, but every analogy has its limitations, including that one. Marriage isn't just a frame to set off the picturesque relationship.

Logian   So what else is it?

Big G   Tell me if this is going to get too uncomfortable, Theo, but could I perhaps use your own experience as an example?

Logian   Well, I wouldn't agree to just anybody doing that, but I'm willing to trust you.

Big G   That's good of you, Theo. If more people said that, I could really change the world. So: it's no secret of course that you and Fiona had a rather tough time a few years ago – and, if you'll allow me to say so, earned a lot of respect for the way you handled it.

Logian   It didn't seem that way at the time, though: reporters camping on the doorstep, nasty, speculative reporting in the tabloids. In fact, that's why we eventually decided to go public: so we could tell it our own way.

Big G   And can you remember what both of you said?

Logian   If I remember rightly, something terribly pompous and moralistic about marriage vows being sacred and we were determined to keep them.

Big G   Fine. And don't apologise for it – it really did my heart good to hear it. So the ceremony and the legalities actually provided a kind of anchor, did they?

Logian   A grab handle, more like.

Big G   So for you at that time, the marriage ceremony wasn't a mere legal obligation; it was something to hang onto when the going got rough.

Logian   Yes, I suppose it was.

Big G   A source of strength in a crisis.

Logian   Yes.

Big G   A means of grace, even? A kind of sacrament?

Logian   Yes, you could say that.

Big G   That's good, Theo. Because that was my intention when I gave it to the world. I'm glad you appreciated my gift.

Logian   Well, that's it for tonight. Thanks for watching; see you next week: eleven o'clock, on the dot, *On the Spot*. Goodnight.

Slightly Smaller G

Logian Good evening and welcome once again to *On the Spot*. This is supposed to be the time when I put someone in public life in the hot seat and give them a good grilling, so to speak. For the last few weeks, though, I seem to have been on the receiving end. Apart from anything else, I'm never too sure what form my guest will take. God of Surprises is one well-known description, and tonight it's especially apt. Please welcome Big – or perhaps for tonight Slightly Smaller – G.

Big G 'Ello, Mr. Logian.

Logian Big G, it's very nice to have you here. Would you like to explain to all the nice people out there why you've come here tonight as a little boy?

Big G Are you alright, Mr. Logian?

Logian Yes, thank you. Why do you ask?

Big G Well, your voice 'as gone all funny.

Logian Funny?

Big G Yeah.

Logian Can you be a little more specific, please, Big G?

Big G Okay. Well, sorta patronisin'.

Logian Who are you calling *patronising*?

Big G	That's better. You 'ad me quite worried there, Mr. Logian. For a minute, I thought you were goin' to pat me 'ead.
Logian	I'm sorry, Big G. I didn't intend –
Big G	's OK. No problem. Want a lick o' this? It's t'rific!
Logian	No, thank you. I don't eat lollipops. In fact, I'm surprised that you do.
Big G	Somethin' worryin' you, Mr. Logian?
Logian	Well, I don't really have a problem with your appearing as a child –
Big G	Just that you expected me to be'ave a bit diff'rent.
Logian	Different*ly*.
Big G	Sorry, Mr. Logian?
Logian	The word is 'differently'.
Big G	Oh. Grammar.
Logian	These things matter.
Big G	Y'reckon?
Logian	You're not being very polite to me tonight, Big G. Are you trying to tell me something?
Big G	Sorry, Mr. L. Just a bit o' fun; don't take it to 'art. Just that when a lot o' grown-ups are with kids they end up talkin' like Norman Brittas. Now it doesn't bother me much, but some

kids really get put off by it. So I thought I ought to mention it.

Logian   Point taken, Big G. Perhaps we'd better start again.

Big G   T'rific. You first.

Logian   Right. Um, good evening, Big G.

Big G   Evenin' Mr. Logian.

Logian   Perhaps you could begin by explaining why you've chosen to appear in this form tonight?

Big G   Not the first time. 'cept last time it took longer, 'cause I started as a baby an' worked up to it.

Logian   Yes, I've often wondered . . . actually, this could be a great opportunity to fill in a few gaps. Tell me, just what sort of child were you?

Big G   'ow d'you mean?

Logian   Well, for a start, did you drop your aitches then, as well?

Big G   No. I spoke Aramaic then, an' there's better ways of bein' dead common.

Logian   It's just not quite the image I had.

Big G   Get real, Mr. Logian! My mum was married to a carpenter, not a scholar.

Logian   Not all carpenters drop their aitches.

Big G   True, but that one did. Or at least e would 'ave if 'e'd been English but 'e wasn't so 'e didn't.

Logian	Fair enough, Big G. But I'm sure all the mummies and daddies out there –
Big G	'ey! Less of the Joyce Grenfells.
Logian	Sorry. I expect the parents out there would find you a wonderful example to their children – if you could just give us a bit more detail.
Big G	What d'you know already?
Logian	Only the story about Jesus getting lost in the temple.
Big G	Yeah. Bit silly that, but there you go – just wandered off an' got lost. Got it in the neck for it, later, an' all.
Logian	Well, perhaps we'd better not dwell on that one, then.
Big G	That's alright, Mr. Logian. You ask whatever you like.
Logian	It does seem like a less than perfect thing to do, doesn't it?
Big G	What? Wand'rin' off alone in a strange city? I should say so, Mr. Logian.
Logian	Not a very good example to modern children.
Big G	Too right. But no kid's perfect.
Logian	What! Even if he's God? This is most bizarre!
Big G	Seems to me the Bible talks about learnin' obedience. Everyone 'as to do it. Part of bein' really 'uman, I guess.

Logian	And that's all the information we have about your earthly childhood. Why isn't there any more?
Big G	Why d'you think? 'Cause it's *borin'*, that's why. Just growin' up like any other kid, gettin' into scrapes, bein' got out of 'em, bit o' duckin' 'n' divin' . . .
Logian	Sounds exciting to me. Not boring at all.
Big G	Yeah, but any kid could tell the same story.
Logian	OK, Big G, but would you perhaps like to say what was the most important thing to you?
Big G	Yeah, if you like. A good 'ome 'elps, but even then it's strange bein' a kid. Most grown-ups are t'rific. Treat you like a real person, know what I mean? But some just don't try to understand. An' that's 'orrible. If there's one thing really gets to me it's seein' parents an' children not gettin' on. Poor little perishers don't stand a chance if their folks aren't int'rested. Sorry, Mr. Logian.
Logian	That's alright, Big G. Would you like a tissue?
Big G	No. 's alright, I've got my sleeve.
Logian	I don't think that's a very good example to set to other children, is it?
Big G	Oh, well, if you want *that* kind of good example you don't want me. You want Hymie bar-Zebedee.
Logian	Who?

Big G   Nice little chap, 'e was. Lived a couple o' doors away. Only thing wrong with 'im was that there was nothin' wrong with 'im. Know what I mean, Mr. Logian? I tell you, if niceness 'ad been 'orses 'e'd 'ave run a livery stable. Always bein' 'eld up as a good example to the rest of us. Made 'im very unpopular. Pity, that. I liked 'im lots.

Logian   What happened to him?

Big G   Very sad. Gave 'imself a nervous breakdown. Somehow got the nickname of 'Legion', Mr. Logian. Took a miracle to set 'im straight. You sure you don't want a lick?

Logian   No, thank you.

Big G   Suit yourself. Still, 'e finished up alright in the end. Nice, that.

Logian   So you don't actually want children to be good, then?

Big G   Depends, dunnit?

Logian   On what?

Big G   Well, *ev'rybody* should be good: love each other, be'ave considerate, all that stuff – and if you correct my grammar again I'll *really* get childish – but some grown-ups don't always mean that.

Logian   We don't? I mean, they don't?

Big G   Glad you agree, Mr. Logian. No, what they sometimes mean is, 'Don't get in the way', 'Don't ask awkward questions' – that sort o' thing.

Logian	I think you might be being a little ungenerous there . . .
Big G	I offered you two licks o' my lollipop!
Logian	Yes, of course, I'm sorry.
Big G	's alright. Like I say, most grown-ups are t'rific, really. It's just that they get all panicky when children are around in case we run riot an' they can't stop us. 'course, once we get wind o' that, it's all the more likely. If they'd just relax, we'd gen'rally be'ave alright.
Logian	Perhaps now would be a good opportunity to talk about children in the Church?
Big G	Great! Fire away.
Logian	Right. So what is the place of children in the Church.
Big G	Why do they need a place o' their own?
Logian	Because children do have particular needs, for which we have to provide.
Big G	So do old folk, but you don't put 'em into sep'rate rooms.
Logian	No . . .
Big G	Somethin' wrong? Somethin' botherin' you?
Logian	It's just that I thought I saw something moving in your pocket.
Big G	Oh, don't worry about 'im.

Logian	'im? I mean – him?
Big G	Pet snake. Wanna 'old 'im?
Logian	*[Shrinking away]* No, thank you. Some people might be a little surprised at you carrying a snake around with you.
Big G	Nothin' wrong wi' snakes. Got a bit of a bad press for a while, but they're smashin', really. 'specially this one. I call 'im Pavarotti.
Logian	Pavarotti?
Big G	Yeah. 'cause of 'is scales.
Logian	Well, I just hope he's under control.
Big G	Do me a favour! What do you think?
Logian	Let's get back to this question about children and the Church.
Big G	Churches are like parents, really.
Logian	You mean that children need to be cared for and supervised?
Big G	You're pullin' my leg, Mr. Logian!
Logian	No, I'm not. Oh! Pavarotti! Scales! I've got it! It was a joke. *[Falls about with exaggerated laughter]* I'm sorry. Now, what did you mean about churches being like parents?
Big G	's obvious, innit? There's good an' there's bad. Some parents 'ave children 'cause they really love 'em, but some think they own kids – toys for adults to play with – so they don't let 'em grow up.

Logian	You may have a point.
Big G	Then there's the others.
Logian	Others?
Big G	Confused people. Can't tell the diff'rence between children an' insurance.
Logian	Insurance?
Big G	Yeah. For their old age.
Logian	Oh, I see. So you're saying that churches do those things as well.
Big G	Some do. 'specially the last one. 'Children are the Church of tomorrow.'
Logian	And you want children to be more involved in the Church *today*?
Big G	Why not? 's what we are.
Logian	So you approve of all-age worship?
Big G	'course I do. It's wicked!
Logian	Wicked? Oh, of course.
Big G	C'mon. Mr. Logian! Where's your street cred?
Logian	I don't believe in it.
Big G	Oh, witty! You should be on telly.
Logian	Thank you; I'll tell the producer. To return to my question: if I understand you correctly, you want children involved in the general life of the Church?

Big G	's right.
Logian	But surely, we all have to learn, and the children are at a different level from adults.
Big G	Sure. But 'ow're you ever goin' to improve if you don't mix with us?
Logian	I walked slap into that one, didn't I!
Big G	Didn't you just, Mr. Logian! No disrespect, o' course.
Logian	Absolutely. And I do accept the serious point that children have things to teach us, but even so, grown-up worship isn't easy for children to understand.
Big G	Worship's like riding a bike. Can't learn without doin'.
Logian	No, but you wouldn't learn by cycling on the M25.
Big G	Too right, I wouldn't. 'ave you seen 'ow folk drive on that road? It's like Russian roulette wi'out the safety precautions. Would *you* ride a bike on there?
Logian	No, but you know what I mean.
Big G	Worship doesn't 'ave to be like drivin' on a motorway, does it?
Logian	No, of course not.
Big G	*Worship* can be quite interestin' –
Logian	Certainly –

Big G	'course, it can get dead dull. Like the M25 on a bank 'oliday – everyone sittin' there staring at the back of the 'ead in front an' tryin' not to nod off.
Logian	But children wouldn't understand a lot of what goes on in church.
Big G	No. You're right there. Then again, some of the grown-ups can't, either.
Logian	Well . . .
Big G	Go on, Mr. Logian. Tell the viewers what you said to Mrs. Logian last Sunday – when you were drivin' away from church.
Logian	Oh, yes. Well, that was a rather untypical example. I don't think it would be helpful to –
Big G	Cut the flannel, Mr. Logian. Tell 'em – I dare you!
Logian	Dare me? You know me too well, Big G! I expressed some lack of clarity in my comprehension of what had been said.
Big G	That wasn't exactly 'ow you put it, but it'll do.
Logian	Well, yes, I was a little uncertain –
Big G	You were completely lost, an' so was everyone else.
Logian	Yes, you're quite right of course.
Big G	Yeah, well, don't worry. So was I. An' so was the preacher. 'e'd been so carried away with 'is philosophisin' 'e'd lost track of 'imself.

Logian	Then I think you've just proved my point. It's a good thing the children weren't there or they'd have been *completely* out of it.
Big G	Maybe. On the other 'and, if children'd been there, 'e'd've 'ad to keep it simple. And 'oo knows, 'e just might 'ave said somethin' worthwhile.
Logian	But the point is –
Big G	Point is, Mr. Logian, adults don't understand some o' the time, any more than children. Just 'cause they've been around longer doesn't mean they actually know any more.
Logian	I suppose not. But I still don't see how it would really work.
Big G	You read in bed, don't you, Mr. Logian?
Logian	Yes I do. Why?
Big G	You goin' to tell ev'ryone what you're readin' now?
Logian	I'm sure they don't want to know that.
Big G	Well, let's just say you've 'ad that copy for a long time.
Logian	Yes, that's true. I have.
Big G	So you liked that book when you were a kid?
Logian	Yes – but I didn't understand it the way I do now, of course.
Big G	So let me get this straight, Mr. Logian –

Logian Forgive me for interrupting, Big G, but if you don't want the rest of that lollipop –

Big G 'ere you are, then. I knew you wanted it, really.

Logian No, I meant, would you like me to throw it away for you?

Big G No, thanks. I'll save it for later. *[Puts remains of lollipop into his pocket]*

Logian Can we get on?

Big G What? Oh, yes. So you 'ad a book when you were young like me – an you liked it. An' now you still like it?

Logian Yes, but on quite a different level.

Big G Same words, though, innit? Same stories, same characters.

Logian Yes, but –

Big G So if you read that story to children an' parents together, they might all enjoy it?

Logian Yes.

Big G An' understand it?

Logian Yes, but on different levels. So you're saying it should be possible to worship on several levels at once?

Big G Sure. Not easy, mind, but possible. I'm always willin' to 'elp. 'ere, are you alright, Mr. Logian?

Logian   What? Oh, yes, thank you. Just feeling rather
               tired for some reason.

Big G   'course you are, Mr. Logian. It's been an 'ard
               evenin' for you. If you can just pass over
               Pavarotti, I'll be goin' now.

Logian   Pavarotti?

Big G   Yes. 'e sneaked into your jacket pocket a
               minute ago.

               *[On hearing this, Logian, overcome by panic,
               removes his jacket and flees from the set]*

Big G   Oh, that's a shame. I'd better go an' look after
               'im! I s'pose I'd better finish off for 'im, first,
               though. Thanks for watchin'; see you next
               week. Eleven o'clock, on the dot, *On the Spot*.
               G'nite! C'mon, Pavarotti. Let's go 'ome.

Fragrance of Heaven

Logian	Good evening and welcome to another edition of *On the Spot*. I must begin by apologising for the delay in starting the recording. I'm afraid it's one of the ever-present risks with a live audience: a guest is late arriving and we have little choice but to wait. It seems very strange to me that Big G, of all our guests, should be late but that is in fact the case. Don't worry about the sounds offstage: our security service is having a little trouble ejecting a gentleman of the road who appears somehow to have got in. I'm sure they'll soon have the situation under control, and then possibly our guest . . .

[Enter Big G, dressed as a tramp]

Big G	Hello, Theo. Boy, did I have a hard time getting here!
Logian	What? Oh, surely not!
Big G	Are you alright, Theo? You look very pale.
Logian	It *is* you, isn't it!
Big G	Yes, but it's no thanks to those security guards of yours.
Logian	Well, perhaps they didn't recognise you.
Big G	That's quite possible. May I sit down?
Logian	Wouldn't you like to . . . take a shower, first. I'm sure the audience wouldn't mind waiting.

Big G   You've got a problem with honest sweat, have you?

Logian   That rather depends on how much of it there is.

Big G   Which is probably why some of my room-mates find it so hard to get in anywhere.

Logian   Your *room-mates*?

Big G   Oh, yes. Although to be strictly accurate, I should say my cardboard-box-mates. We share everything you know: food, money, influenza . . .

Logian   Livestock?

Big G   Sometimes. All part of creation's rich tapestry, you know.

Logian   I presume you've arrived like this to make a point?

Big G   Well, not entirely. I mean you wanted to interview me – the *real* me. And that means that I come in lots of different shapes and sizes.

Logian   Not to mention fragrances. I'm beginning to realise that. But do you have to *stay* in that one?

Big G   Oh, I think I should. It's one of the manifestations I particularly like.

Logian   So how much of your time do you spend like that?

Big G   All of it.

Logian   No you don't. You've never looked like that before when I've seen you.

Big G   Haven't I?

Logian   No. You've been other things – like a woman . . .

Big G   That's the wonderful thing about omnipresence. I can be manifest in all possible forms, all the time. Leaving that aside, though, I don't really think you should refer to women as 'things'.

Logian   Just a figure of speech, Big G. Anyway, the point is that you've appeared here as a woman, as a schoolboy, and as a man, but you've never appeared as a tramp before.

Big G   Not on this show, you're right. But of course I don't only appear here, do I?

Logian   Point taken, but I'm talking about this show.

Big G   And *I'm* talking about King's Cross station at half past six yesterday evening.

Logian   Of course: I remember you now. I didn't know that was you!

Big G   All the more credit to you, then.

Logian   Sorry?

Big G   Well if you didn't realise who I was, your reaction does you all the more credit. It's not often somebody stands up for me in that way.

Logian   Yes, well – the things that other chap was calling you were quite unnecessary.

Big G   That's true.

Logian   And besides, 'Go forth and multiply' is your line, not his.

Big G	Yes, but I'm not going to get petty about that. Anyway, he wasn't such a bad chap, you know. If he hadn't just been told his job was in jeopardy –
Logian	Yes, now that's something I've always wondered. Where is that place?
Big G	What place, Theo?
Logian	Jeopardy. Where all the jobs are?
Big G	Oh, I see. About a couple of miles from Hand – where all the tasks are.
Logian	Perhaps we'd better get back to the subject in – the subject we were discussing.
Big G	Yes, while we've still got some viewers.
Logian	So where were we?
Big G	Talking about the chap at the station last night. He's really a smashing sort, you know. It's just that like many people he finds beggars a threat because he feels helpless. And that sometimes makes him angry and he takes it out on us. It's not unusual.
Logian	And I suppose, to be fair, some people who beg *are* threatening – literally.
Big G	That's true, but I'm not happy about that as a reason for avoiding the issues. It's wrong for anyone to intimidate others for their own ends, and that applies equally to beggars, bankers and business executives.

Logian	I take your point. Of course, a lot of people won't give money to beggars – and you know the reason why.
Big G	Because they know what we'll spend it on.
Logian	Exactly.
Big G	And our friend last night would probably say that too, and mean it. And I quite understand his point of view. The only problem with that, of course, is where he went after he'd called me all those names.
Logian	Now there you have the advantage of me, Big G: I've no way of knowing that.
Big G	Well, while you were so kindly buying me that cup of tea from a hot dog stand, he was in the bar enjoying a whisky and soda. Not that I begrudge him it in the slightest, mind you; it just seems a little inconsistent when he'd refused to give money to a tramp in case it got spent on the same thing.
Logian	I suppose he'd say that he drinks responsibly.
Big G	Yes, actually he does; what a pity he makes such blanket assumptions about other people.
Logian	Well . . .
Big G	And in any case, what gives the rich the right to decide how the poor should spend their money? You must admit it seems somewhat presumptuous for the haves of society to expect the have-nots to be non-smoking teetotallers, especially when they themselves are often neither.

Logian   But we all have to make choices according to
our consciences, don't we? I mean, I don't
give money to certain charities, because I don't
approve of the way they spend it. And I don't
invest money in funds that benefit arms
manufacturers. So in the same way, that man
had every right to choose where to donate his
money, and he might have decided that, for
example, cancer relief was a better choice than
paying for someone's drink habit.

Big G   Yes, and he might well be right. Obviously,
you had the same concern, didn't you – that
you might be paying for my drink habit, that
is. And I don't blame you, as far as that goes.

Logian   That's why I bought you a cup of tea.

Big G   And a hot dog, Theo. Don't forget the hot dog.
You know, people might think of me as a bit of
a traditionalist, but there's something rather
special about a really well-prepared hot dog –
nice spicy sausage, lashings of ketchup, eaten
out of soggy greaseproof paper. Love it!

Logian   I'm a cheeseburger man myself, I must admit.

Big G   Yes, I know. It was fun, wasn't it?

Logian   To be honest, I don't think I've enjoyed myself
so much for quite a long time – putting the
world to rights over a burger and a polystyrene
mug of tea. It was a really good conversation,
considering . . . whoops, sorry!

Big G   Considering I was a tramp. You'd be amazed
at the people you can meet down there. The
woman next box but one to mine has a PhD in

economics – used to have a high-flying job in the City. You'd love talking to her.

Logian   Why's she on the streets?

Big G   Credit card debt. Never could balance the family budget. But you ought to meet her, though, she'd give you some interesting angles on society.

Logian   You must introduce me sometime.

Big G   Certainly. You know, people who push past street beggars don't know what they might be missing.

Logian   Well, with respect, there's one thing they *can't* miss, can they? I mean, put it like this: it's OK at a hot dog stand in the open air, but I couldn't have sat with you in a restaurant looking and smelling like that.

Big G   Very considerate of you, Theo, but I really wouldn't have minded.

Logian   That's another one I walked into feet first!

Big G   Have you never heard the phrase 'the fragrance of heaven', Theo?

Logian   I'd never imagined it to be like that!

Big G   No, and neither had the people at a church I visited last Sunday. The preacher was praying that the 'fragrance of heaven' should fill his church. I must say I find the language a little strained, but each to his own. Anyway, that was what he wanted. The 'fragrance of heaven'.

Logian   Oh, you didn't!

Big G   Well, he'd asked, hadn't he? So in I went. And I had more trouble with the door stewards there than I just did with your security chaps. I suppose they found the fragrance of heaven overpowering.

Logian   Yes, I imagine they did. Or, at any rate, not quite what they'd expected.

Big G   Yes, well, for a while I began to regret going in.

Logian   Why was that?

Big G   Didn't seem any point in being there, really. If I want fiction I can always pop over for a chat with Jane Austen.

Logian   Fiction?

Big G   Well, it wasn't about any world *I* recognised, anyway. I think the minister thought he was talking about heaven: a bizarre sort of place full of people with nothing to do, who apparently had earned their ticket there in some sort of rat race of a previous life. If he hadn't kept saying what good people they'd been, I'd have thought he meant the House of Lords.

Logian   So did you put him straight?

Big G   Oh, no, it would have been unkind to embarrass the poor chap like that.

Logian   You've never been so reticent with me.

Big G   Oh, come now, Theo. I've never gratuitously embarrassed you, and anyway, you're a professional interviewer and we've discussed the ground-rules. This would have been quite different.

Logian   Fair enough. So what *did* you do?

Big G   What everybody else was doing. I sat and listened.

Logian   You didn't announce yourself?

Big G   Now that would have caused a stir, wouldn't it? A dirty tramp sitting at the back of the church and heckling. 'Sorry, vicar, you've got it all wrong – oh, and by the way, I'm God, so I should know.' Not that I've never said that sort of thing, but no one's ever believed me, anyway.

Logian   I see what you mean – but I'd have loved to have seen it, though.

Big G   Well, I'm not saying I don't get pushed out of churches from time to time, but I prefer not to provoke it if it can be avoided.

Logian   So you just sat there?

Big G   Yes – it's a way I often like to work. You'd be amazed what I can achieve by just being there. And in this case it worked a treat.

Logian   Tell me more!

Big G   After the service ended, most of the congregation trooped through to another room for coffee. It smelt very good, I can tell you, but I wasn't really very keen on it.

Logian   Why, if it smelt so good?

Big G   Because it wasn't fairly traded coffee, and I knew what the working conditions of the coffee pickers were like – but that's another story. Anyway, I never go for coffee unless I'm invited. So I just stayed at the back of the church and looked round. There was a petition on the table about the derelict house some of my friends are living in just down the road. They wanted it knocked down to clean the area up. Well, I just stood and read it, and that was when the Big Event happened.

Logian   What was that?

Big G   It was one of the congregation. I know her, of course – the Right Honourable Mrs. Amelia Fotheringaye-Smythe.

Logian   What about her?

Big G   Well, she was just looking for her custom-made solid gold pen, to sign the petition, when she saw me. Perhaps my disguise wasn't up to much, but I swear she saw through it. All of a sudden she got really angry, tore up the petition and came over to me, all smiles.

Logian   And don't tell me: she hugged you?

Big G   Good mortals, no! That would have been a miracle even by my standards. No, she shook my hand, thanked me for coming and said she hoped I'd be there again. Then came the best bit. She started asking about me. Really interested, she was – wanted to know my name, whether I'd got any family, how I was coping with the cold weather, all that kind of thing. It's a long time since anyone ever showed that kind of genuine interest in me. I don't mind telling you, I got quite overcome for a few moments.

Logian What happened next?

Big G Well, then it got *really* exciting. The whole place was alive with angels, singing and dancing like there was no tomorrow. A right old celestial rave up, and if I hadn't known better I'd have sworn they were on something.

Logian But they weren't?

Big G Do you mind! Well, I suppose they were. It's called joy.

Logian Joy in heaven – which of course is why only you knew about it.

Big G I think my friend Mrs. F.-S. knew. She's a terrific woman, you know, as long as you get past the high society stuff to the real her.

Logian And what about the rest of the church? Did they realise what had happened?

Big G Not straight away, but by the time Amelia's finished with them they'll know what heaven's *really* about. And in all kinds of little ways they'll start to get involved. They're a grand crowd, you know; just need a bit of a nudge now and then.

Logian   And a change of vicar, perhaps?

Big G   Oh, no, you mustn't misjudge him. I went to see him a few months back, and he recognised me straight off.

Logian   Really!

Big G   Well, not literally, but he was very good to me.

Logian   So why didn't he recognise you on Sunday?

Big G   I looked different, that first time. I wasn't a beggar; I was a pregnant teenager with parent problems. I don't mind telling you he was really kind. Of course if he was strictly honest he didn't approve of me very much, but he sorted things out for me really well. And he *listened*, which was more than most people were doing then.

Logian   I must say *I* find the idea of your being a pregnant teenager pretty difficult to handle.

Big G   So do a lot of people – most, even. It's easier for them to see me in the kind of folk they can sympathise with, but we're back to that omnipresence thing again. I'm in everybody, all of the time, whether socially acceptable or not. I say, Theo, can you smell anything strange?

Logian   No, I don't think so.

Big G   There you are, then. You've even stopped noticing that. Once people get to recognise me they generally stop worrying so much about the externals.

Logian	That's fine, but I know this is you. I mean, *really* you. What about when it's not?
Big G	It's always me, Theo, but sometimes you've got to look pretty deeply into the person to find me. Mrs. Amelia Fotheringaye-Smythe knew that, for all her social position.
Logian	So what you're saying is that people have got to meet you in beggars –
Big G	In *anyone* they're afraid of, Theo. It might be beggars, but it might equally be all kinds of other people. I'm always there.
Logian	What, in everyone?
Big G	Everyone.
Logian	Were you in Adolf Hitler?
Big G	Yes, but I got buried pretty deep in that particular instance. It was mainly when he was with one or two particular people – and his dog – that I managed to break through occasionally.
Logian	What a better place the world would be if people had been able to recognise you there!
Big G	The world would have been an even better place if *he* had been able to recognise me there.
Logian	And on that note, we have to close. Thanks for watching; see you next week: eleven o'clock, on the dot, *On the Spot*. Goodnight.

The Servant God

Logian   Good evening and welcome to another edition of *On the Spot*. I'm afraid that once again our guest is late arriving, and the recording is being held up. No doubt there is some purpose in this delay, of which we may learn later. Perhaps while we're waiting –

[Enter Big G in the form of a cleaning woman, with feather duster and vacuum cleaner]

Logian   I'm sorry, you can't come in here, we're about to do a recording.

Big G   That's alright, dear, don't mind me. I'll just plug this in here, shall I? Pick up your feet for me, there's a love. Don't worry, I'll soon be done. Can't have a programme going out from a dirty studio, now can we? Whatever would the Broadcasting Standards Authority say about that, eh, dear?

Logian   Look: there's an audience out there; we're waiting to start a recording. *You are going to have to do this later!*

Big G   Oh, bless you, dear, I don't mind if they watch. There! All done, now, dear. Ooh, my knees! You don't mind if I sit down a minute, do you?

Logian   Well, I'm very sorry about your knees, but that chair's for a particularly important guest.

Big G   Yes, dear.

Logian   I don't think you understand. This studio is in use. I'm Theo Logian.

Big G   I know, dear.

Logian   Oh, no! Don't tell me you're –

Big G   Big G, dear. Pleased to be here again, I'm sure.

Logian   I can't cope with this.

Big G   Are you alright, dear? You look a little peaky to me.

Logian   Yes, I think I'm fine.

Big G   You need more greens in your diet, dear.
               It's the iron, you know.

Logian   Yes, I imagine it is. Big G, why – I'm not sure whether I dare ask this question – *why* have you come here like this tonight?

Big G   Seemed like a good idea, dear. That carpet was a disgrace, and I thought, 'Well, I'm not going to broadcast from a dirty studio – I'd better go and clean it up', and here I am.

Logian   Yes. You've clearly got into the character, but do you need to keep up the act?

Big G   Act, dear? Act? This is no act; it's really me.

Logian   But surely, you can't be all these different people?

Big G   Oh, bless you dear, I can be lots more than that. And I am. All the time. I mean, I wouldn't want to leave anybody out, now would I? But don't worry, dear, you just ask your questions.

Logian   Let me get this straight. You're not appearing *as* a cleaner. you really *are* a cleaner.

Big G   No, dear.

Logian   Ah. As I thought.

Big G   No, *[pointing to vacuum cleaner] that's* a cleaner, dear, and with what this company are making they could afford to get me a better one, I don't mind telling you. 'Industrial Grade Corporate Cleanliness Consultant' is what *I* am.

Logian   Corporate Cleanliness Consultant?

Big G   *Industrial Grade,* dear. I'm the heavy duty version – which is more than that poor old vacuum cleaner can say for itself: capable of twenty-four hours' continuous use, that's me.

Logian   I'm very sorry.

Big G   Don't be, dear, it's only a title after all. No need to be overawed by it – you just carry on calling me Big G.

Logian   Of course, I'd always known *in theory* that you were willing to humble yourself –

Big G   Humble myself? I'm not sure I'm with you, dear.

Logian   Perform menial tasks.

Big G   Nothing menial about this, dear. Why, I remember the days when a whole studio could be brought grinding to a halt because Mr. Dibbleton's chair hadn't been dusted.

Logian   Yes, of course. I didn't mean to upset you.

Big G   Oh, love you, dear, I'm not upset. But tell me, how many different jobs do you do?

Logian   Well, I interview people of course – or sometimes they interview me – and I help a bit with the research.

Big G   And very important work it is, too, dear. But it's not very technical, is it?

Logian   I beg your pardon?

Big G   D'you know how many different kinds of disinfectant there are?

Logian   No, actually, I don't.

Big G   So you won't know what the results of using the wrong one might be?

Logian   I've got a feeling you're going to tell me.

Big G   Oh, no, dear. You can't cover all that in a few minutes. What I can tell you, though: *[leans forward in her chair as if confiding a delicate piece of information]* you remember that time when the newsreader read the news standing up?

Logian   Yes. I've always wondered about that.

Big G   Well, there you are, dear. Very unfortunate mistake – although it had its funny side, I must say. That's the problem with work experience people, you see. They haven't any work experience.

Logian	So you're saying there's no such thing as menial work, then?
Big G	Put it this way, dear: if we had washrooms in heaven –
Logian	I know. I'd be down for cleaning them.
Big G	Oh, no, dear! Well, not at first, anyway. You have to work up to a job like that.
Logian	Yes, of course. So this is what is meant by the first being last and the last first?
Big G	Not really, dear. That was more to do with your marginalised people, if you know what I mean. Domestic engineers aren't marginalised.
Logian	No?
Big G	Bless you, no, dear. We're right at the heart of things, we are. All doors open to you when you've got a bucket and mop in your hand. I mean, you're a pretty senior chap round here, aren't you, dear?
Logian	That's nice of you to say so.
Big G	Not at all, dear, you deserve your success. It's just that, well, you haven't got a key to the Director General's office, have you, dear?
Logian	No, and I suppose you have?
Big G	That's right, dear. And they give me a mobile phone as well.
Logian	I've been trying to get one of those for years, but they don't believe I need one.

Big G   Well, there you go, dear. But of course I've got a very responsible job, and they sometimes need me really urgently. I mean, some programmes get very messy, you know.

Logian   So let me get this straight. You've got free access to the DG's office, and a company mobile telephone? And I can't even get a reserved parking space.

Big G   Really, dear? Well you can use mine whenever you like; I don't often drive to work.

Logian   It seems to me they treat you like a star.

Big G   Like a star? Oh no, dear; I get very good treatment here. No complaints.

Logian   That wasn't entirely what I meant.

Big G   Would you like me to put a word in for you, dear? William's a lovely man, and he always listens to what I say.

Logian   William? Oh, you mean Sir William – the Director General?

Big G   That's the one, dear. You leave it to me, and I'll see if I can't get a mobile phone for you.

Logian   That's very kind of you. I must admit I'm a bit taken aback by all this.

Big G   Don't mention it, dear. Glad to help.

Logian   No, I mean by your appearing in this way tonight.

Big G   Oh, love you, dear, don't let it worry you. We
             corporate cleanliness consultants are quite
             approachable, really. They all know me, you
             know – all the presenters and the producers.
             Why there's hardly a week goes by without
             someone asking me to sign something or other.

Logian   You sign autographs?

Big G   No, dear, requisition forms, but it's all part of
             a day's work.

Logian   And what else do you do?

Big G   Well, let's see, I sometimes take a turn on the
             car park entrance when they're short, and last
             night I stood in for the concessionaire on the
             main door. It's his feet you know, but I'm
             going to get them seen to for him.

Logian   So you're everywhere, then?

Big G   Everywhere, anywhere, all the time, dear.
             Some people call me ubiquitous.

Logian   What does the U stand for?

Big G   *Ubiquitous*, dear, from the Latin 'ubiquitas' –
             present everywhere. But I prefer 'omnipresent'
             – makes me sound a bit less like a Volkswagen
             Beetle.

Logian   Oh, I don't know; in some ways it seems
             quite a good analogy. Reliable, not showy –
             humble even. I used to own one, actually.

Big G   Ah, well, there you are, dear – that's the
             difference.

Logian	That nobody owns you? Some people seem to think they do.
Big G	Always a problem, dear, but it happens. There is something else, though.
Logian	Something else?
Big G	About Beetles. If you've had one, you'll know. People who like them seem to like each other, as well.
Logian	That's true. If ever I was in trouble I only had to stand near the car and the next one along would stop to offer help.
Big G	That's nice, dear.
Logian	I've forgotten where we were, again.
Big G	Ubiquitous, dear. I'm always around.
Logian	Yes, I think you've got a point. I'm going to have to be a little more polite to people from now on.
Big G	Oh, you're alright, dear. Now tell me, how's that lovely wife of yours – Fiona?
Logian	Don't you know already?
Big G	Well, yes, dear, but it's nice to ask, don't you think? D'you mind if I slip out of these shoes for a minute? That's better. You know this job really gets you under the arches. Now where was I? Oh, yes. Fiona.
Logian	She's very well, thank you. And so are the boys.

Big G   Oh, love them! They're such little bundles of mischief, aren't they? Tell me, how's Dan getting on with that new teacher at school? Had a few problems at first, didn't he, dear?

Logian   Yes, but why are you asking me? If you're everywhere, and all seeing, you don't need me to tell you.

Big G   Bless you, dear, if everyone thought like that no one would ever pray! Of course I know, but it's nice to talk. Shows that we care, doesn't it?

Logian   So is that what prayer really is? Just a case of chatting with you about things you already know?

Big G   Well, I must admit I do like a good natter, dear, and most people don't bother, just because they think that.

Logian   And that's all that it's about?

Big G   Bless you, no, dear! It's how I like to work. If you think about it, I could clean this whole building on my own, no problem. But I don't, dear. I like to have people working with me. Dan getting on better at school now, is he?

Logian   Yes, since you ask. I had a brilliant idea about that, and finally got it sorted. He gets on really well with that science teacher now.

Big G   What was the brilliant idea, dear?

Logian   Really, it was a stroke of luck. I heard that the teacher liked photography. So I suggested to Dan that he showed him some of *his* photographs.

Big G   The wildlife ones.

Logian   Yes. And then they had something positive
               to share together instead of the teacher just
               criticising all the time.

Big G   That's right, dear. I'm really glad it worked
               out well.

Logian   Just a minute. Are you saying that was all
               your idea.

Big G   Oh, love you, no, dear! We talked about it.
               Don't you remember?

Logian   I don't remember ever praying about that.

Big G   Not *as such*, dear, but it was when you were
               really worried about it and you talked it over
               with that nice Jane Enfield.

Logian   The English teacher. Yes, and she just
               happened to mention the photography in
               the conversation.

Big G   That's right, dear. I think the three of us made
               a good team, don't you?

Logian   But I wasn't praying, then.

Big G   Yes you were, dear. Leastwise, I heard you.

Logian   So you're saying that everything is prayer,
               because you can always be involved.

Big G   That's right, dear. But I do like the other kind
               as well, you know. I'm very good at
               eavesdropping, but it's nice to talk face to
               face, isn't it?

Logian   Even when the conversation isn't quite what one expects. Big G, I must thank you very much once again for being my guest. And to all of you, thanks for watching; see you next week: eleven o'clock, on the dot, *On the Spot.* Goodnight.

Also from Kevin Mayhew

Act One and Act Two
MICHAEL FORSTER

Each book contains 45 Bible dramas ideal for use in all-age worship. Stories from the Old and New Testaments have been imaginatively rewritten while retaining and emphasising the original meaning. The dialogue is deliberately modern in order to make the characters as recognisably like real people as possible, rather than dim figures from the distant past, speaking in conventional religious language. *Act One* and *Act Two* mix sound teaching with humour and valuable insights and, as with all good writing, the dramas communicate on many levels.

Take 10
RAY JACKSON

These ten discussion dramas are designed for use in youth groups to encourage members to explore social and ethical issues such as the environment, euthanasia, homelessness and poverty, to understand the decisions faced by those in authority, and to explore the Gospel message in a way which they will find relevant to their everyday lives and the society in which they live.